What Can She Be?
A NEWSCASTER

What Can She Be?
A NEWSCASTER

**Gloria and Esther Goldreich
photographs by Robert Ipcar**

Lothrop, Lee & Shepard Co./New York

Lothrop *What Can She Be* Series
What Can She Be? *A Veterinarian*
What Can She Be? *A Lawyer*
What Can She Be? *A Newscaster*

Our thanks to the management and staff
of WINS radio, the management of WNEW-TV
and the staff of "Black News."

Text Copyright © 1973 by Gloria Goldreich and Esther Goldreich
Photographs Copyright © 1973 by Robert Ipcar

Printed in the United States of America.

Library of Congress Catalog Card Number 73-4940
ISBN 0-688-41540-7   0-688-51540-1 (lib. bdg.)

For our mother Gussie Goldreich

This is Barbara Lamont. Barbara is a newscaster for both radio and television in New York City. A newscaster is someone who reports the news. By listening to Barbara's broadcasts and watching her telecasts, people can find out what is happening in their city.

Barbara may tell her listeners about a fire or about a new animal at the zoo. Sometimes she tells them about a problem in a neighborhood. Sometimes she reports to them on a new school or park. Her job is to tell her listeners about the interesting and important things that happen every day.

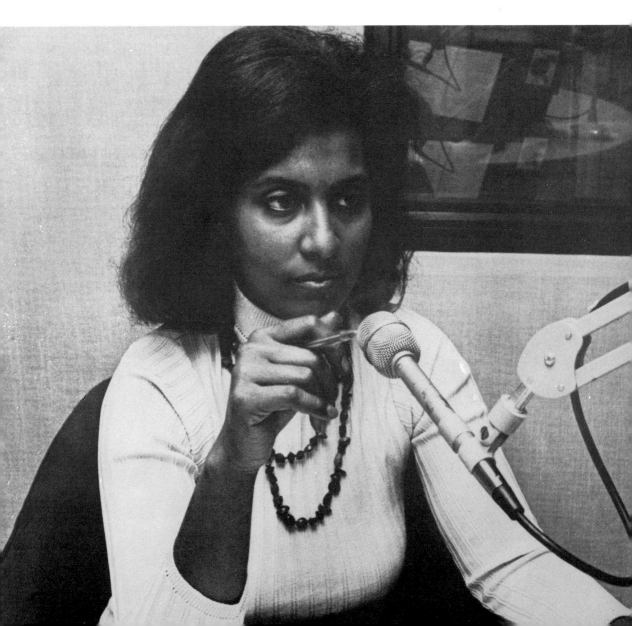

Mornings are a busy time for Barbara and her family. Before she leaves for work she and her husband help Michael and David, her two older children, get ready for school.

She talks to Gina, her household helper, about what must be done that day. David tells Barbara that he will listen to her program that afternoon. Michael, David, and Lisa are proud when they turn on their radio and hear their mother's voice report a news event.

Barbara's first stop is at her radio station. She talks to Marge, the news editor, about the plans for the day. They discuss what is most important and what Barbara will cover.

A group of people have complained about the condition of the pavement and benches on an uptown mall. A press conference will be held there with city leaders. Barbara will cover this story first.

Carrying a small, compact recorder with its attached microphone, Barbara hurries uptown. Many other journalists are at the outdoor press conference. These conferences are often held when some group wants to tell the public about something important. Newspapers, magazines, radio, and television stations are asked to send reporters to hear what is said.

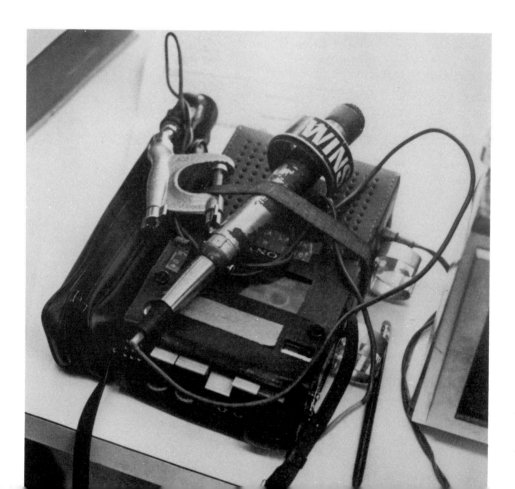

Barbara interviews some city leaders about the mall. She asks them many questions. They answer and explain the problem.

While they talk, construction workers arrive to make the needed repairs. Barbara talks to one of them. She records her conversations. Later, these tapes will be played in the radio station for Barbara's listeners in their homes.

Back at the studio, Barbara listens to her tapes while she writes a narration. The narration helps her listeners understand what her interviews are about. She chooses the most interesting parts of the tape for her radio report.

Carl, the sound engineer, makes a small cartridge of each part. Barbara then goes into a sound-proof studio. She adds her narrative to the recorded interview on one large cartridge. This finished cartridge then goes to Marge who sees that it is played as soon as possible.

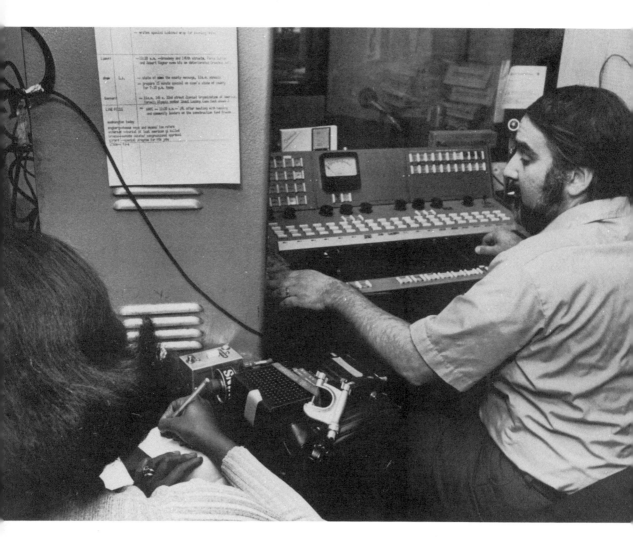

All radio stations receive mail from their listeners. Sometimes people write to a newscaster about a problem. Hank Simon, the news chief, shows Barbara a letter. It is from an old man who is having a hard time collecting some money that is owed to him. He thinks he might have an easier time if Barbara's listeners heard about his problem. Barbara thinks his story is interesting and interviews him at his apartment.

The old man is shy but because Barbara is friendly and knows how to ask the right questions, he soon begins to talk about his problem. Good reporters try to understand the feelings of the people they are interviewing. If people feel at ease, they will talk in a relaxed way and give all the facts.

One day a week Barbara films a television show. The show will be telecast a few days later. Filming for television is harder than taping for radio. There is much more equipment. Cameramen, technicians, and a production coordinator all go with Barbara to her television interviews. Before they set out, they check their schedule.

Their first stop is at the National Urban League. Barbara interviews a man who wants to help veterans who have just come back from the armed services. In his office, he tells his plans to Barbara. Both he and Barbara wear small microphones around their necks. While they talk, the cameraman is filming, the sound technician is taping, and the bright television lights are shining. The Urban League office has become a television studio.

The man tells Barbara that many veterans want to go to college but do not have the chance or the money. He hopes that Barbara's television viewers will write to the government and ask for more help for veterans.

The next stop is an uptown branch of the New York Public Library. This branch houses a collection of Black historical objects and papers. The collection is large enough to be put into a museum. For five years, the library has been asking the city for a new building. Barbara talks about this with the librarian. The television cameras roll.

Later in the week, Barbara and a technician edit the film. They choose the best parts to use on the show. Barbara makes some phone calls to check her facts. Reporters spend a lot of time on the telephone, making sure that what they tell people is so.

26

Barbara writes the narration for her interviews. She reads it to the production coordinator and a staff writer. They tell her their feelings. Then she knows if her story is clear. She wants her broadcast to be as interesting as possible to her audience.

Everyone who is on television wears special make-up. Here, a make-up man works on Barbara's face, while she makes last minute changes in her narration.

There is time before the show starts for a talk with a fellow worker about a problem. Everyone is glad to have Barbara's ideas. Because they work so closely, people on television and radio often become friendly.

Suddenly everyone becomes quiet. "Black News" is ready
to be taped.

The news is always changing so no two days in the life of a news reporter are alike. On a quiet afternoon, Barbara's friend Amy brings her two nieces from Wisconsin to the studio. Nora and Jenny are lucky. Barbara has some time to show them around.

She shows them the offices and the special sound-proof studios. They meet the anchorman. It is his job to read the headlines and to introduce and arrange the newscasts and the taped interviews. Nora wants to know why the anchorman is wearing earphones. Barbara explains that they help him to hear his own voice while he speaks. The anchorman at the radio station in Wisconsin wears earphones too, she says.

There are many clocks in the studio that tell the time in cities and countries all over the world. When it is night in New York, it is afternoon in Africa. An African newscaster may be ready with an important broadcast. Perhaps a newscaster has told the New York station that something important will happen in London at noon. A look at the London clock tells the news editor in New York that it is time to tune into London for that story.

The girls are very excited by their tour. Their friends at home will hear many stories about Barbara's radio station.

After Nora and Jenny leave, the news editor asks Barbara to ride around the city in a car that has a mobile microphone. The car also has a two-way radio. While Barbara is inside, she can talk to the people in the studio and they can answer her. Today they ask her to go to Central Park.

There has been some vandalism. Benches are broken, shrubbery is uprooted, and trash cans are overturned. The news editor wants Barbara to find out how the people who use the park feel about the vandalism.

36

"Whenever I see someone tearing up a plant or picking a flower I ask them to stop," one young man tells Barbara. "If everyone did that there would be no beautiful things growing in our park."

"We all try to pick up trash wherever we see it," a girl says. "A clean city is a healthy city. A clean park is a beautiful park."

Barbara tells the young people that her radio audience will be glad to know that there are many people who care about their city.

Barbara loves her job because it gives her a chance to meet many kinds of people—rich and poor, young and old. One afternoon she visits a workshop where older people do work for large companies. In this workshop, people are putting together pencils and compasses that will be sold to school children.

An old woman in a wheelchair is one of the fastest workers. "Let me know when the program will be on the air. My grandchildren will want to listen," she explains. Barbara promises.

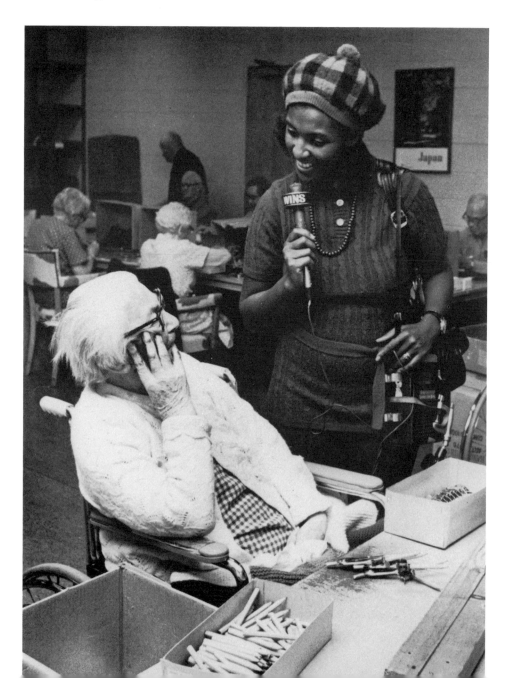

Back at the studio, Barbara edits the tapes, writes her narration, and records the program. She is glad that she taped the interviews.

Many people want to know what is being done for old people. A reporter chooses stories that are important and interesting to listeners.

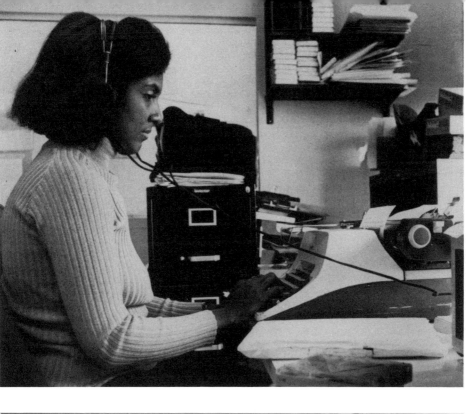

At the end of the day Barbara is tired but she has a good and happy feeling. Her family is waiting for her. After dinner she checks the children's homework and hears about their adventures and her husband's day at work.

She tells the children about some of the things that she did during the day. Michael, David, and Lisa love their mother's stories. They often tell their friends about her work. Many of their friends and even their teachers, listen to Barbara on radio and watch her on television.

When the children are asleep, Barbara and her husband settle down to an evening together. Because she is interested in flying, Barbara reads a book on it. Some evenings she reads books and articles that help her with her work. She is even writing a book herself.

Barbara loves being a newscaster. Every day is different. She is always meeting new people and learning new things. She thinks newscasting is the best kind of work for her to do.